NONFICTION
COMPANION

TO

Pam Muñoz Ryan's

Esperanza Rising

Lisa Kurkov

Rourke
Educational Media

BEFORE, DURING, AND AFTER READING ACTIVITIES

Before Reading: Building Background Knowledge and Academic Vocabulary

Before Reading strategies activate prior knowledge and set a purpose for reading. Before reading a book, it is important to tap into what your child or students already know about the topic. This will help them develop their vocabulary and increase their reading comprehension.

Questions and activities to build background knowledge:
1. Look at the cover of the book. What will this book be about?
2. What do you already know about the topic?
3. Let's study the Table of Contents. What will you learn about in the book's chapters?
4. What would you like to learn about this topic? Do you think you might learn about it from this book? Why or why not?

Building Academic Vocabulary
Building academic vocabulary is critical to understanding subject content.
Assist your child or students to gain meaning of the following vocabulary words.

Content Area Vocabulary
Read the list. What do these words mean?

- asylum
- boycott
- capitalist
- drought
- Dust Bowl
- dust storm
- fiesta
- immunity
- Okies
- repatriation
- spores
- strike

During Reading: Writing Component

During Reading strategies help to make connections, monitor understanding, generate questions, and stay focused.
1. While reading, write in your reading journal any questions you have or anything you do not understand.
2. After completing each chapter, write a summary of the chapter in your reading journal.
3. While reading, make connections with the text and write them in your reading journal.
   a) Text to Self – What does this remind me of in my life? What were my feelings when I read this?
   b) Text to Text – What does this remind me of in another book I've read? How is this different from other books I've read?
   c) Text to World – What does this remind me of in the real world? Have I heard about this before? (news, current events, school, etc.)

After Reading: Comprehension and Extension Activity

After Reading strategies provide an opportunity to summarize, question, reflect, discuss, and respond to the text. After reading the book, work on the following questions with your child or students to check their level of reading comprehension and content mastery.
1. What prompted so many immigrants from Mexico in the 1930s? (Summarize)
2. Why do you think Isabel was not chosen as Queen of the May? (Infer)
3. Why did laborers go on strike? (Asking Questions)
4. Esperanza longs to celebrate her quinceañera. What do you celebrate? (Text-to-Self Connection)

Extension Activity
Esperanza has to make the decision where or not to go on strike. Do some deeper research on the California labor strike in the 1930s. What decision do you think you would have made?

TABLE OF CONTENTS

About *Esperanza Rising* and Pam Muñoz Ryan 4

The Mexican Revolution. 8

The Phoenix 12

Queen of the May 14

Quinceañeras 16

The Zapotec 18

Food 20

Oklahoma Farmworkers. 24

Strike! 28

Valley Fever. 32

Dust Storms 36

Mexican Jamaicas and Fiestas 40

Discussion Questions. 44

Writing Prompts and Projects 45

Glossary 46

Bibliography and Index 47

About the Author 48

ABOUT *Esperanza Rising*

and **Pam Muñoz Ryan**

The inspiration for the main character in *Esperanza Rising* was Pam Muñoz Ryan's grandmother. Although Ryan knew that her grandmother had worked in a farm camp, she didn't realize until later that her grandmother's early childhood in Mexico was much like Esperanza's—filled with servants, pretty dresses, private schools, and other luxuries.

Esperanza Rising tells the story of Esperanza, who must leave the comfortable, well-to-do life she has always known for a new life in America. Everything changes a great deal after Esperanza's father is killed. She must learn to live as a farm laborer in the San Joaquin Valley, sharing a small house, babysitting, doing physical labor, and deciding if she should go on **strike** with other laborers.

Women of Strength

Ryan enjoys telling the stories of strong women, both real and fictional. In her picture book, Amelia and Eleanor Go for a Ride, *Ryan wrote about two famous women, Amelia Earhart and Eleanor Roosevelt, who snuck away from a White House dinner to take a ride in a plane. When* Marian Sang *shares the life of Marian Anderson, a Black singer who broke racial barriers with her music.*

Ryan grew up in Bakersfield, California, in the San Joaquin Valley. She uses the San Joaquin Valley as the setting for most of *Esperanza Rising*. Her half-Mexican heritage influences many of the books she writes, and she has won the Pura Belpré Award twice (for Latino/a authors and illustrators who portray the Latino cultural experience in their writing).

Ryan had lots of free time as a child to play and develop her imagination, which she believes helped her become a writer. She also moved when she was in fifth grade and felt like she didn't fit in. Ryan became an obsessive reader, in part because it was an escape from her unhappiness at school. Little did she know that one day, she'd become the author of more than 40 books herself!

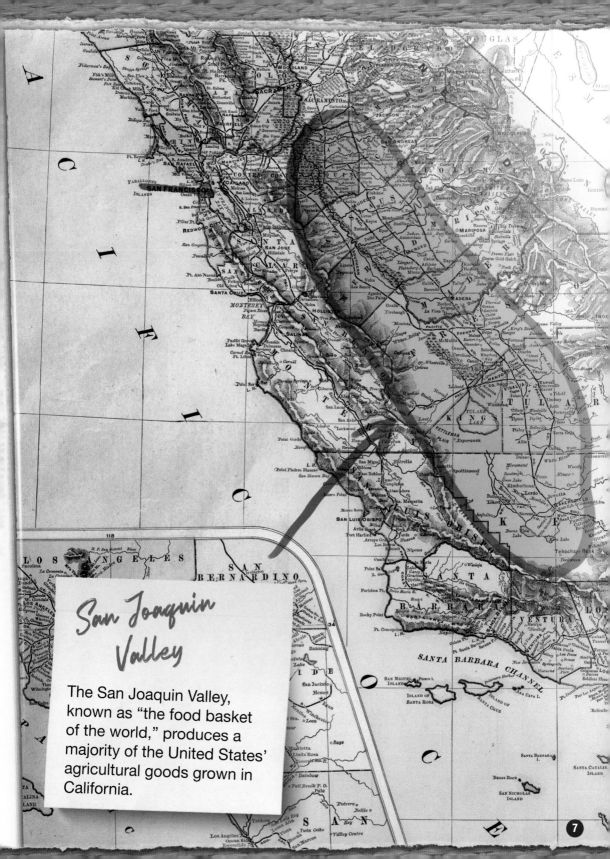

San Joaquin Valley

The San Joaquin Valley, known as "the food basket of the world," produces a majority of the United States' agricultural goods grown in California.

THE MEXICAN REVOLUTION

From the Novel

Marta, a young farmworker, says that her father fought in the Mexican Revolution. Her tone sounds accusing when she adds that her father fought against landowners like Esperanza's family. Esperanza feels defensive and responds that her father was a good man who gave property to his servants.

The Mexican Revolution began in November of 1910. The ruler at that time was a dictator named Porfirio Díaz. His goal was to create a **capitalist** society. But peasants and farmworkers suffered as he focused on building new factories, roads, and dams, and creating a modern society.

Díaz also created new land laws that benefitted only the wealthy. Small farmers, who felt that they had no other options, lead the revolt. Over the next seven years, many new Mexican presidents came and went. The country remained unstable, and much of the population remained unhappy.

In 1917, the Constitution of Mexico was created. Although this was viewed as the official end to the revolution, fighting continued. The war was over long before the majority of *Esperanza Rising* takes place, but the farming class's bitter feelings toward the landowning class still existed.

Presidency in the Revolution

Sept. 1910 Porfirio Díaz becomes president for eighth term

May 1911 Francisco León de la Barra becomes interim president

Nov. 1911 Francisco Madera becomes president

Feb. 1913 Victoriano Huerta becomes president

Oct. 1915 Venustiano Carranza becomes president

Oct. 1920 Alvaro Obregón becomes president

THE PHOENIX

From the Novel

The day before Esperanza leaves for America, Abuelita reminds her of the story of the phoenix. The bird rises from its own ashes and begins life anew, which is what Esperanza and her mother will have to do.

The legend of the phoenix is ancient and has appeared in Greek, Roman, and Egyptian mythology. The phoenix was said to be a large bird, like an eagle, with colorful feathers and a musical call. Only one phoenix existed at a time, and it lived for about 500 years. When the magnificent bird's end approached, it would build a nest and then set the nest on fire. A new phoenix would rise from the ashes, which represented rebirth for many people.

QUEEN OF THE MAY

From the Novel

Isabel desperately hopes to be chosen Queen of the May at her school. The best girl student is picked to dance around a pole with colored ribbons on May Day. Isabel is not chosen. Unfairly, the honor always goes to a blonde, blue-eyed girl, never to a Mexican girl.

The Queen of the May is a girl who leads the procession at a May Day parade. She usually wears white to symbolize purity, and she often gets to wear a crown or tiara. May Day is celebrated on May 1 to welcome the change of seasons and honor workers' rights. May Day celebrations are still popular in England and Canada.

Many maypoles use colorful ribbons and flowers.

Maypole

The maypole dance is performed on May Day. During this 600-year-old British tradition, a tall pole is hung with greenery, flowers, and ribbons. The dancers dance in circles, often weaving patterns with the ribbons. The dance and weaving of ribbons symbolize the lengthening of days as summer gets closer.

QUINCEAÑERA

From the Novel

Although Esperanza is a couple of years away from her **quinceañera**, she and her friends talk and dream about it. It is a rite of passage into womanhood, but it is also a party, complete with fancy dresses, favorite foods, and an extensive guest list.

For a girl who is about to turn 15, a quinceañera is a major event. It traditionally has two parts—the mass, or religious service, and the **fiesta** or party. Shoes play a symbolic role in the church ceremony. The girl arrives in flats, which are a symbol of her childhood. Her father gives her high heels to change into, which symbolizes her adulthood.

Sweet 16

In the 1930s, a quinceañera meant that a girl was old enough to date, then marry and start her own family. Social norms have changed, and today's celebration is more of a tradition than anything else. Girls today are often eager to celebrate an American "sweet 16," so sometimes the family holds a party that combines the two celebrations.

THE ZAPOTEC

At the beginning of the novel, we learn that Hortensia, the family's trusted housekeeper and nanny, is Zapotec. She and her husband, Alfonso, are described as having dark skin and being of small stature. They are close friends and companions to the family, and help Esperanza and her mother escape to America.

The Zapotec civilization reached its peak around 500-700 AD.

Monte Albán, formerly a great Zapotec city, is now an important archeological site.

The Zapotecs, also known as the "Cloud People," are the largest indigenous group in Oaxaca, where Hortensia is from. More than 64 Zapotec languages have evolved over thousands of years! Ancestors of modern-day Zapotecs were known for farming (including corn, beans, squash, tomatoes, and chocolate), as well as hunting and fishing.

Dancers still reenact Zapotec history during the Guelaguetza Festival in Oaxaca, Mexico.

FOODS

Once they move to California, Esperanza's family eats simple, fresh foods, like tortillas, beans, rice, vegetables, and fruit. When Esperanza reminisces with Isabel about her life back in Mexico, she tells stories about the elaborate Christmas meals they had, including *empanadas*, *tamales*, and hot chocolate.

Tamales have corn-based *masa* or dough, wrapped around a filling, and steamed in a corn husk.

Much of the foods that we think of today as being traditionally Mexican are actually Tex-Mex—Mexican foods adapted by Texans of Mexican descent using ingredients more readily available in the U.S. such as cheddar cheese, beef, wheat, and cumin. Traditional Mexican food has its roots in Mayan, Spanish, and Aztec cultures.

Guacamole

Guacamole, a popular avocado dip, is an authentic Mexican dish created by the Aztecs. The original recipe used only avocados, but modern versions have evolved to include other ingredients like onions, tomatoes, and spices.

- *one tomato, chopped*
- *¼ cup diced onion*
- *one large, ripe avocado*
- *2 T lime juice*
- *a pinch of salt*
- *¼ cup cilantro, chopped*

Cut the avocado in half and squeeze the insides into a bowl. Discard the pit. Use a fork to mash the avocado until it is smooth. Stir in the lime juice and salt. Add tomato, onion, and cilantro. Gently fold into avocado mixture. Serve with corn chips for dipping.

Traditional Mexican foods often center around beans, vegetables (particularly tomatoes, corn, and chile peppers), rice, and tortillas. The tortillas tend to be made of ground corn instead of flour. Seafood is popular near the coast, and chicken and pork are more common than beef.

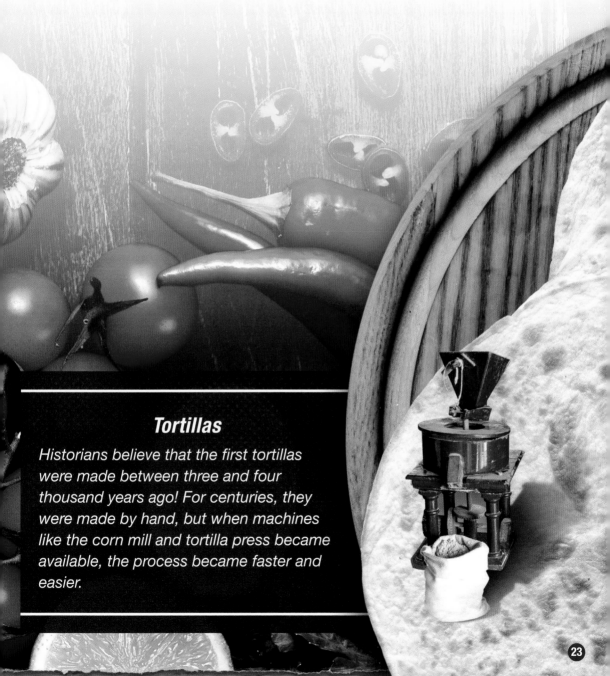

Salsas are also an important part of Mexican cuisine. A simple salsa can be made from fresh chopped tomatoes, tomatillos (similar to green tomatoes), peppers, and cilantro. Mexican food is known for its bold flavors. Traditional spices, such as achiote, epazote, allspice, chile powders, and more, are used to round out dishes.

Tortillas

Historians believe that the first tortillas were made between three and four thousand years ago! For centuries, they were made by hand, but when machines like the corn mill and tortilla press became available, the process became faster and easier.

OKLAHOMA FARMWORKERS

From the Novel

Esperanza experiences the competition for work between the Mexican farm laborers and "Okies," or migrant workers from Oklahoma and other nearby states. At one point, Esperanza is dismayed to learn that the Okies will be moving to a new company camp, where they will have indoor toilets, hot water, and a pool.

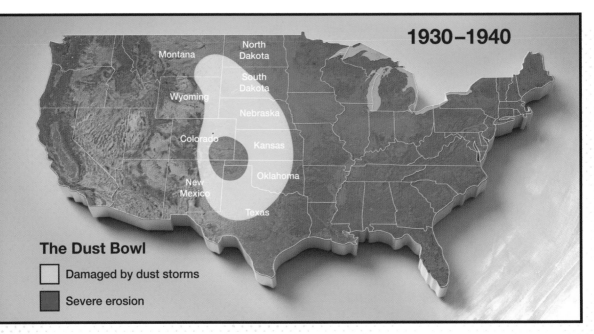

1930–1940

Montana
North Dakota
South Dakota
Wyoming
Nebraska
Colorado
Kansas
New Mexico
Oklahoma
Texas

The Dust Bowl

☐ Damaged by dust storms

◼ Severe erosion

During the Great Depression, people from Oklahoma (as well as Texas and Arkansas) began traveling West to California in search of farm work. They came from an area of the Midwest nicknamed the "**Dust Bowl**." The combination of a long-lasting **drought** and overgrazed and overworked land created a major crisis.

Grapes of Wrath

In 1939, author John Steinbeck published a novel called The Grapes of Wrath *about the fictional Joad family. They lose their Oklahoma farm and head west to California in hopes of finding a better life. Instead, they face new challenges and difficulties. The novel was an instant success and was later followed by a Hollywood movie.*

People were anxious to move to California, particularly the very productive San Joaquin Valley. At the time, the area supplied about 25 different types of produce to the country's grocery stores! Such a place provided a beacon for Oklahomans who were just about out of hope.

Many of the people who moved West were not actually farmers; they had just heard stories about crops that needed harvesting in California. They were usually white and often moved as a family. The migrants were disappointed when they arrived to find a shortage of work, and they were forced to accept meager wages.

Dorothea Lange

Dorothea Lange was a photographer who was well known for the photos she took documenting the Great Depression. Lange's pictures were often of people otherwise forgotten in society: the homeless, the unemployed, migrant workers, families who traveled looking for work, and sharecroppers. She included descriptions of what she saw, as well as the words of the people she photographed.

STRIKE!

Fairly soon after Esperanza's family arrives at the farm camp, Esperanza starts hearing rumors about a strike. Miguel is surprised and asks Marta if she doesn't need the work. She replies that of course she does, but that the Mexican workers may have the power and ability to create change if they band together.

When Oklahomans started pouring into California looking for work, they drove down the wages. There was a huge pool of workers to choose from, which meant that companies could pay much less, and there would always be someone hungry enough for work to take the job.

White government officials claimed that the large unemployment rolls in California were Mexican and Mexican American farmworkers. But this wasn't true. The largest number of unemployed were white migrants from other states, desperate for work during the Depression.

Mexican workers banded together, often with other people of color, to protest low wages and conditions that were getting worse and worse. The government responded with **repatriation** plans, meaning they could send "troublemakers" back to Mexico. Even if they were legal U.S. citizens of Mexican heritage who had never been to Mexico, they could still be sent there if they participated in protests or strikes. In the U.S., people of Mexican heritage still face racism. **Asylum** seekers, migrants, and U.S. citizens of Mexican descent, including children, can be held in detainment centers, and families can be separated.

No Grapes!

*César Chávez grew up as a migrant farmworker in California during the Depression. In 1962, Chávez and Dolores Huerta organized a labor union called the National Farm Workers Association. Chávez was known for leading protests that brought attention to the plight of migrant farmworkers. He got Americans to **boycott** California grapes and led a strike of California grape pickers that lasted five years!*

César Chávez ends his hunger strike with Sen. Robert Kennedy.

VALLEY FEVER

From the Novel

Esperanza is very worried when her mother is diagnosed with Valley Fever. The doctor explains that most people who live in the area have built up an **immunity** to the infection, but newcomers, especially adults, often become ill.

Valley Fever "Cocci" Infection

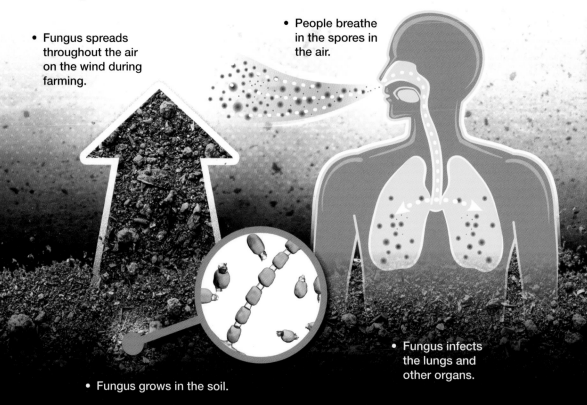

- Fungus spreads throughout the air on the wind during farming.

- People breathe in the spores in the air.

- Fungus infects the lungs and other organs.

- Fungus grows in the soil.

Valley Fever is an infection caused by a fungus found in the soil of dry, desert areas of the American Southwest, as well as parts of Central and South America. The **spores** of the fungus have long filaments. When they are disturbed—by farming, construction, or even the weather—the filaments break off and become airborne. The wind can carry Valley Fever spores hundreds of miles!

A damp cloth or dust mask can help protect against the spores.

Symptoms of Valley Fever include a fever, cough, rash, chills, fatigue, joint aches, and night sweats. In milder cases, the patient gets better fairly quickly without much treatment. In severe cases, like Esperanza's mother's, the condition can turn into pneumonia, and recovery can take months.

Some simple precautions can help lessen the risk of getting sick. The chances of becoming ill are higher in the summer. Wearing a mask outdoors can help, as can staying inside during dust storms. If you need to work with the soil, wetting it first can prevent the spores from becoming airborne.

DUST STORMS

Esperanza has no idea what is happening when she encounters her first **dust storm**. The sky darkens, and the wind covers everything with sand and dirt. She is babysitting with Irene and Melina, who tell Esperanza to stay away from the windows and help her stuff rags under the door to keep out the dust.

A dust storm is a cloud of tiny dust and sand particles that have been swept up by the wind. The storms can be enormous, stretching for miles. Life pretty much comes to a standstill during a dust storm. The tiny particles make breathing impossible, and everything is obscured by dust, the way it would be by snow in the middle of a blizzard.

THE DUST BOWL

Black Sunday

Black Sunday is a dust storm that occurred on April 13, 1935, in the Great Plains—the center of the Dust Bowl. The temperature quickly fell more than 30 degrees Fahrenheit. The wind whipped up a massive cloud of dust hundreds of miles wide. The storm lasted for hours, creating panic and fear. It is believed to have moved 300,000 tons of soil!

Dust storms take place in dry, arid locations. They happen in deserts, like those found in the Southwest or the Middle East, or they can occur in places that have been affected by **drought**. Dust storms often are accompanied by cold fronts and thunderstorms. The air that pushes through an area before a storm stirs up the small, dry particles, causing them to rush into the air.

Dust storms also increase the spread of disease around the world. Virus spores are blown into the atmosphere, where they combine with air pollution. When the particles drop back down, people inhale them, which causes many problems, from dry eyes to pneumonia.

MEXICAN JAMAICAS AND **FIESTAS**

From the Novel

In the summer, jamaicas, or fiestas, are held on Saturday nights. These informal parties are a chance for the Mexican workers to have a break, enjoy life a little, and remember traditions from home. There is music, dancing, food booths, and bingo, and people gather from other camps and even other towns to enjoy themselves.

Life as a farmworker was difficult, and there was little opportunity for recreation or relaxation. The weekly fiestas were a reminder to laborers of a different life—better times before the Depression or perhaps an easier life at home in Mexico, surrounded by family and tradition.

In Mexico, fiestas are held for a variety of reasons. There are religious fiestas to celebrate saints, fiestas to celebrate the harvest or the rainy season, and even fiestas for civic holidays. Parades, music, and fireworks may be part of the celebration, as well as bullfights, rodeos, or carnival rides. People often dress in colorful, traditional clothes or costumes.

In Mexico, there are fiestas for every month of the year—as well as smaller, local ones that occur across the country. Independence Day is one of the most important holidays. It occurs on September 16th and commemorates the Mexican fight against 300 years of Spanish rule. Like other fiestas, parades, fireworks, music, and food play a significant role.

Day of the Dead

One of the most well-known Mexican celebrations is Día de los Muertos, *or Day of the Dead. On November 1st and 2nd, loved ones who have died are honored. Altars, called* ofrendas, *are decorated with photos, candles, food, small gifts, and other offerings. For a short video, search* Day of the Dead *and* National Geographic *on YouTube.*

DISCUSSION QUESTIONS

1. How did Ryan's childhood experiences help her become a writer?

2. Have you eaten Mexican food before? If so, describe what you've had. If not, share some traditional Mexican foods you would like to try.

3. What was the purpose of the farmworkers' strikes?

4. How are American celebrations similar to Mexican fiestas?

5. Do you think Ryan would have been able to write Esperanza's story as well if it had not been based on her grandmother's life? Why or why not?

6. Why did people travel West to California in the 1930s?

7. Describe what Valley Fever is and how it spreads.

WRITING PROMPTS AND PROJECTS

1. Find a book of Dorothea Lange photographs in the library, or search for her photos online. Look at the photos and choose one that you find particularly interesting. Write about the picture as though you had been there. Where was it taken? Are you in the photo? What was happening? How did you feel about it?

2. Research the Saharan Dust Storm of 2020 that sent dust from Africa all the way to America. How is it similar to and different from the dust storms of the 1930s?

3. Tortillas are a type of Mexican flatbread. Other cultures have their own flatbreads. Do some research online to find out what sorts of flatbreads are found in other parts of the world. Share their names, their country of origin, and a few words about what they are like.

4. Detailed Project: Explore the author!

   • Visit Ryan's author site (pammunozryan.com).

   • In the bar on the top, click on Readers Theatre Scripts. You'll find scripts for shortened versions of four of Ryan's books, including *Esperanza Rising*. The scripts are for either four or five voices.

   • Choose one and find the appropriate number of friends or family members to read it aloud with you.

   • Take some time to read through your parts and make any helpful notes. Try to make your voices match the characters.

   • If possible, make an audio or video recording of the reading and share it with classmates, friends, or relatives.

GLOSSARY

asylum (uh-SAI-luhm): the protection granted by a nation to someone who has left their native country for safety

boycott (BOI-kot): to refuse to buy or use something

capitalist (KAP-i-tl-ist): a person who supports an economic system in which resources are owned by individuals, not the government

drought (drout): a long period of very dry weather

Dust Bowl (duhst bohl): a region of the Great Plains states that suffered sever drought and dust storms during the 1930s

dust storm (duhst stawrm): a storm with strong winds that fills an area with dust, usually during a drought

fiesta (FYES-tahz): the Spanish word for a festive celebration

immunity (ih-MYOO-ni-tee): the state of having resistance to a disease or an illness

Okies (OH-keez): a slang, often offensive word used to describe farmworkers from Oklahoma who moved West to California during the Great Depression

repatriation (ree-pey-tree-A-shn): the act of sending someone back to the country they came from

spores (spohrz): tiny reproductive bodies, produced by ferns and fungi, among other plants and animals

strike (strahyk): the act of stopping work as a form of protest

BIBLIOGRAPHY

Greenspan, Jesse. "What Happened on Black Sunday?" Last updated April 13, 2020. https://www.history.com/news/remembering-black-sunday.

Kelly, Tracey. *The Culture and Recipes of Mexico*. New York: PowerKids Press, 2017.

Langston-George, Rebecca. *A Primary Source History of the Dust Bowl*. North Mankato: Capstone Press, 2015.

Library of Congress. Immigration . . . Mexican. "Depression and the Struggle for Survival." www.loc.gov/teachers/classroommaterials/presentationsandactivities/presentations/immigration/alt/mexican6.html.

Mayo Clinic. Valley Fever. Accessed July 18, 2020. www.mayoclinic.org/diseases-conditions/valley-fever/symptoms-causes/syc-20378761.

Pam Muñoz Ryan. Accessed July 15, 2020. www.pammunozryan.com.

PBS. History Detectives, Special Investigations. "Mexican Revolution."

Ryan, Pam Muñoz. *Esperanza Rising*. New York: Scholastic Inc., 2000.

INDEX TERMS

Day of the Dead 43
Great Depression 25, 27
Independence Day 43
Mexican Revolution 8, 9
protest 31
quinceañera 16, 17

racism 31
Ryan, Pam Muñoz 5, 6
San Joaquin Valley 5, 6, 7, 26
tamales 20
Valley Fever 32, 33, 34
Zapotec(s) 18

ABOUT THE AUTHOR

Lisa Kurkov lives in Charlotte, North Carolina, where she and her husband homeschool their two children. When her head isn't buried in a book, Lisa enjoys baking, crafting, photography, birding, and adventuring with her family.

PHOTO CREDITS: page 1: Gingagi/ Getty Images; page 1: Christopher Freeman/ Getty Images; page 1: beerphotographer/ Getty Images https://www.shutterstock.com/image-vector/symbol-mexico-black-white-emblem-1030571032; page 1: azerberber/ Getty Images; page 2: cherezoff/ Getty Images; page 2: photoBeard/ Shutterstock.com; page 4: Photo Credit: Mike Brown; page 6: enviromantic/ Getty Images; page 6: Larissa Veronesi/Westend61 GmbH/ Newscom; page 7: nicoolay/ Getty Images; page 8: akg-images/Newscom; page 10: Library of Congress; page 10: grebeshkovmaxim/ Shutterstock.com; page 11: Anastasiia_M/ Getty Images; page 11: AlexLMX/ Shutterstock.com; page 13: Jag_cz/ Shutterstock.com; page 13: Xcages/ Shutterstock.com; page 14: sarradet/ Getty Images; page 14: tonda/ Getty Images; page 14: Staff/Mirrorpix/Newscom; page 15: sarradet/ Getty Images; page 15: Hemera Technologies/ Getty Images; page 16: Shestock Blend Images/Newscom; page 16: Jupiterimages/ Getty Images; page 16: OK ot use- Bisual Photo/ Shutterstock.com; page 17: Jeremy Woodhouse/ Getty Images; page 17 Alex Gorka/ Shutterstock.com; page 18 W. Scott McGill/ Shutterstock.com; page 18 Anton_Ivanov/ Shutterstock.com; page 19 Kobby Dagan / Shutterstock.com; page 20 bhofack2/ Getty Images; page 20 Charlie Neuman/ZUMA Press/ Newscom; page 20 Charlie Neuman/ZUMA Press/Newscom; page 21 Rafael Ben-Ari/Chameleons Eye/Newscom; page 21 etorres69/ Getty Images; page 22 Liliya Kandrashevich/ Shutterstock.com; page 23 zefirchik06/ Shutterstock.com; page 24: kutaytanir/ Getty Images; page 24: World History Archive/ Newscom; page 25: akg-images/Newscom; page 25: Circa Images/Newscom; page 25: sweeann/ Shutterstock.com; page 25: sweeann/ Shutterstock.com; page 26: JT Vintage/ZUMA Press/Newscom; page 27: akg-images/Newscom; page 28: Underwood Archives/UIG Universal Images Group/Newscom; page 29: Dorothea Lange/Heritage Art/Heritage Images AiWire/Newscom; page 30: Everett Collection/Newscom; page 30: by-studio/ Getty Images; page 30: nicoolay/ Getty Images; page 30: UPI/Newscom; page 31: Everett Collection/Newscom; page 32: Captain Wang/ Shutterstock.com; page 32: Yeexin Richelle/ Shutterstock.com; page 32: solar22/ Shutterstock.com; page 32: Aggie 11/ Shutterstock.com; page 32: KATERYNA KON/SCIENCE PHOTO LIBRARY/Newscom; page 33: Dusan Stankovic/Getty Images; page 34: Debra Ferguson/Newscom; page 36: World History Archive/Newscom; page 37: Chris Kridler Cultura/Newscom; page 37: Everett Collection/Newscom; page 37: MARK GARLICK/SCIENCE PHOTO LIBRARY/Newscom; page 38: akg-images/Newscom; page 39: akg-images/Newscom; page 39: Everett Collection/Newscom; page 40: Kobby Dagan / Shutterstock.com; page 40: Kobby Dagan / Shutterstock.com; page 40: Cianto SUN/Newscom; page 41: Igal Jusidman Rubinstein / DanitaDelimont.com "Danita Delimont Photography"/ Newscom; page 41: David Franklin/ Shutterstockc.com; page 42: Kobby Dagan / Shutterstock.com; page 43: Levon Rivers/robertharding/robertharding/ Newscom; page 43: BestStockFoto/ Shutterstock.com; page 43: akg-images/Newscom; cover: Chris Kridler Cultura/Newscom; cover: by-studio/ Getty Images; cover: Andrii Sedykh/ Getty Images; cover: krblokhin/ Getty Images; cover: sassy1902/ Getty Images; cover: rusm/ Getty Images; cover: Tolga TEZCAN/ Getty Images; cover: Tolga TEZCAN/ Getty Images; cover: ANGHI/ Getty Images; cover: Andy Dean Photography/ Shutterstock.com; cover: MARK GARLICK/ SCIENCE PHOTO LIBRARY/Newscom; n/a: enjoynz/ Getty Images; n/a: -slav-/ Getty Images

Library of Congress PCN Data

Nonfiction Companion to Pam Muñoz Ryan 's Esperanza Rising / Lisa Kurkov
(Nonfiction Companions)
 ISBN 978-1-73164-341-4 (hard cover)
 ISBN 978-1-73164-305-6 (soft cover)
 ISBN 978-1-73164-405-3 (e-Pub)
 ISBN 978-1-73164-373-5 (e-Book)
Library of Congress Control Number: 2020945078

Rourke Educational Media
Printed in the United States of America
01-3502011937

Edited by: Madison Capitano
Cover and interior design by: Joshua Janes